EVERY FAMILY IS SPECIAL

By: C Brutus

This book is originally written in English and has been carefully translated into French. Both versions offer the same heartwarming story, ensuring that readers in both languages can enjoy the message.

In a bright little town in Wisconsin, the sound of children's laughter filled the air. Each child had a family, and every family was unique. But not all stories were told as easily as the others.

Dina lived with her mom and dad. They baked cookies together and had movie nights every Friday. But lately, Dina noticed something—her family didn't always seem like the others

Leo lived with just his dad. They went on hiking adventures and built forts in the living room. But one day at school, a classmate asked, "Where's your mom?" The question hung in the air, and Leo didn't know what to say.

Next door lived Daph, who shared her home with her grandparents. She loved the stories they told, but sometimes she wondered why her friends had parents at their soccer games while her grandparents cheered from the sidelines.

Jaden was adopted and lived with two dads. He loved painting and exploring art museums, but at times, whispers followed him in the hallways. "Two dads? How does that work?" they murmured. Jaden stayed quiet, pretending not to hear.

Ama had two moms. They played soccer and cheered at every game, but sometimes Ama caught the strange looks other parents gave. The love was always there, but Ama couldn't ignore the feeling that others didn't understand.

Each child had their own special family, filled with love and laughter, but they started noticing the world wasn't always as accepting. Sometimes, it seemed like they had to defend the very thing that made them feel safest—their families.

On a sunny day, the kids gathered at the park for a family event. While the weather was warm, they felt heavy-hearted, discussing not only happy memories but also doubts and questions weighing on them.

Dina said, "Sometimes I feel like people think my family is too ordinary." Leo nodded, "Someone asked me why I don't have a mom, and I didn't know what to say." Daph frowned, "I get weird looks because I live with my grandparents."

Jaden shared quietly, "People don't understand why I have two dads. It's like they think it's wrong." Ama added, "Yeah, I feel like people judge my moms, and I don't know how to make them see it's okay."

The park fell silent for a moment. Then, Dina spoke up, her voice firm. "Maybe we don't need to make them understand. We already know what matters."

Leo's eyes brightened. "You're right! It's not about what they think—it's about what we know." Daph smiled, "We know our families love us, and that's what's important."

Jaden grinned, "And we don't have to be the same to respect each other. That's what makes it special, right?" Ama's face lit up. "Exactly! We should celebrate it, not explain it."

The group decided to make something special—a poster to show the world what they knew in their hearts. "Families come in all shapes and sizes!" they wrote in bright letters, each child drawing their family with pride.

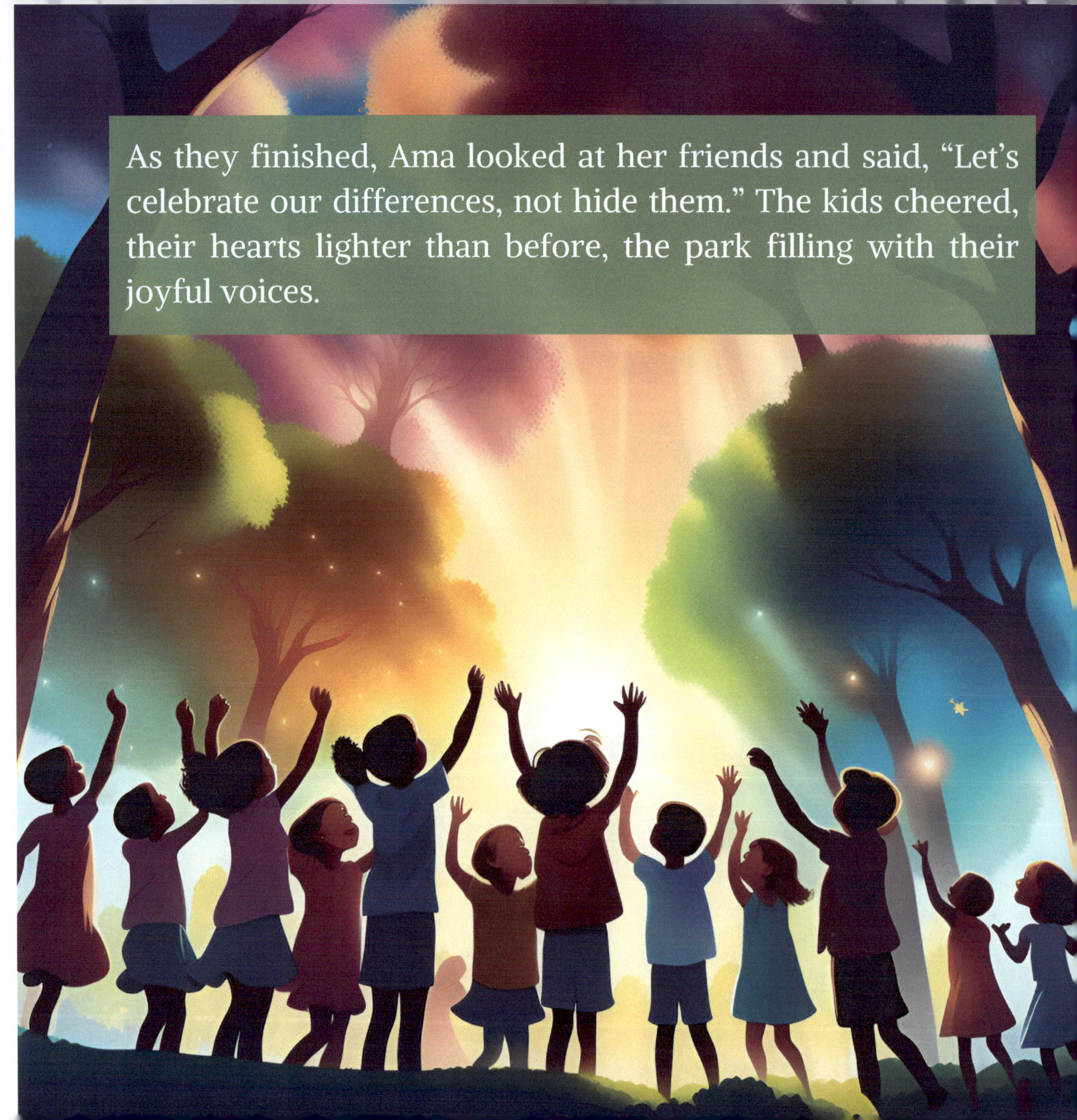
As they finished, Ama looked at her friends and said, "Let's celebrate our differences, not hide them." The kids cheered, their hearts lighter than before, the park filling with their joyful voices.

From that day on, they made a promise. They wouldn't let the questions or strange looks bother them anymore. Instead, they would be proud—proud of the love that held their families together.

No matter how your family is made up—whether you have one parent, two parents, or live with others—every family is special in its own way. In a world that might not always get it, love and respect bring us together. Keep in mind that every child has a story worth sharing with pride.

Draw a picture of your family

I love my family because ________________________

____

____

About the Author

I am C Brutus, I was born in Haiti in October 1992. Upon relocating to the United States, I pursued my education and embraced a diverse range of roles and accomplishments. Balancing the responsibilities of a devoted mother to two daughters and a supportive Navy wife, I handle my family duties with grace and resilience. In my professional life, I work with special education students, showcasing my dedication to inclusivity and education. Beyond the classroom, my love for learning and teaching led me to become a successful author. My collection includes various books like coloring books, activity books, and storybooks, all crafted to engage and inspire young minds. I am truly grateful for your support. A big thank you to my amazing customers for backing my small business endeavors.

Thank you!

C Brutus